Monika Wegler

Dwarf Rabbits

Everything About
Selection, Care,
Nutrition, and
Behavior

Filled with
Full-color
Photographs by
Monika Wegler

BARRON'S

Contents

All About Dwarf Rabbits

Dwarf rabbits are the "minis" among rabbit breeds, and as a result they are particularly well loved as house pets. But every dwarf still has the heredity of its ancestors, the wild rabbits, along with their amazing abilities and qualities.

Getting to Know Dwarf Rabbits

Getting to Know Dwarf Rabbits

Young dwarf rabbits in particular have a positively irresistible effect on children. With their big, wide eyes and their soft fur they look like they were created for cuddling and loving. But rabbits need more than that to be happy: an understanding of their natural behaviors and a chance to live them out. Come with me into the exciting world of rabbits and you will see this lively little housemate in a totally new light.

Happy Only with Other Rabbits

European hares are real loners that get together only at mating time. Wild rabbits, on the other hand, spend their whole life inside their group, which consists of several males and females. If individual family groups get together, they can produce colonies of a hundred or more animals.

The deep-seated need to live together is also innate in our dwarf rabbit. All its behavior is aimed at fitting in as a group animal within the society of other rabbits. Neither centuries of domestication (being kept as pets) nor breeding has succeeded in changing anything that fundamental. It is a widely held misconception that a rabbit kept alone is truly happy. Neither a human nor a guinea pig can replace a rabbit partner. The old saying that a rabbit that's kept alone becomes friendlier is also not true. Often it's the opposite case. This is confirmed by hundreds of letters I have received from desperate owners who have major problems with their single rabbits. Whether the animal forms a trusting relationship with a human, always remains shy, or behaves aggressively usually has totally different causes (see pp. 12, and 50).

Comfort and Enjoyment

Socially oriented rabbits look for and need body contact with other rabbits. They like to lie down together or in a tight, little group and snuggle. Also the animals often press tightly together in stressful situations to feel more secure. In rest periods, sometimes spontaneously, or when one animal nudges another with its muzzle to encourage it, a partner gets licked thoroughly on the head and ears until they exchange places. This social grooming has a calming effect on all participants and solidifies the friendly bonding among rabbits. In sexual contact this licking is stimulating. In my groups there are female rabbits that live with neutered males. I continually observe how rabbits

Of course foot care is no cinch, but anyone who's as flexible as a dwarf rabbit has no trouble mastering the exercise.

lower on the totem pole acknowledge this to the superior (dominant) ones by grooming them frequently. If a dwarf licks your hand or arm, usually while you are petting it, this behavior means, "I like you, so I will groom you."

Who's the Boss Around Here?

There is a strict pecking order in wild rabbit colonies. During mating season, dominant (high-ranking) females in particular aggressively defend their den. And as they reach sexual maturity, the bucks fight violently to determine their rank within the group until one alpha male (the leader of the pack) establishes his superiority. Subordinate rivals flee, so there are no serious injuries. Also, strange rabbits are not automatically tolerated in the territory and accepted into the colony. All these behaviors are important in regulating behavior within the rabbit society. Even our dwarf rabbits display this behavior to various degrees, depending on their individual characteristics. When territorial disputes arise and a gentle "cuddle bunny" suddenly turns into a "fighting rabbit," most owners react with horror and dismay. And that all too quickly is the final blow against social togetherness, for "The rabbits don't get along. They have to be kept apart or given away." If we get into the reasons in a conversation, it quickly becomes clear that misunderstandings, lack of knowledge, and improper living conditions have allowed the whole situation to escalate. The lively little rascals

Are you really part of my family? The sniff test provides the proof; anyone who doesn't smell like family has to keep moving . . .

Hiding in the tall grass is one way to divert attention to something else and wait until the danger has passed.

really can get into a lot of nonsense, and yet they don't deserve to be punished for behaving like rabbits.

How Rabbits "Talk"

To avoid misunderstandings with dwarf rabbits, it's helpful to know how to understand a little bit of "rabbit."

Sitting up: As soon as something captures the rabbit's attention, it assumes an upright body position. This gives the animal a better view of the surroundings.

Rolling: "I feel really good. A box filled with sand would be super."

Nudging: Rabbits greet each other by gently nudging one another with their noses. When a dwarf rabbit nudges you, it means, "Hello, here I am. Do you have a moment for cuddling?" See also page 10.

Nudging your hand away: "That's enough patting. I want to take a break."

Circling your foot: Have you already noticed that your rabbit circles your feet? This behavior is part of the mating ritual. The rabbit circles around its chosen partner. Is your male dwarf rabbit still living alone? Then have him neutered and get him a wife. Otherwise the dwarf will only be sexually frustrated.

Rabbit Characteristics

GNAWING Because their teeth grow continually, rabbits nibble on nearly everything.

DIGGING Rabbits love to dig. In the wild they dig underground tunnels.

MARKING Rabbits are very territorial. They mark, and cannot be counted on to become thoroughly housebroken.

Anatomy and Senses

Nose

A HUNDRED MILLION scent cells enable rabbits to perceive the tiniest scent molecules. We speak in words, but they "speak" with one another through scent messages. For rabbits it is also important to mark their territory.

Eyes

A 360-DEGREE field of view enables rabbits to keep track of their entire surroundings, even overhead. In addition they see well in poor light conditions. This enables rabbits to detect enemies quickly and flee.

Whiskers

WHISKERS ARE in the area of the nose and mouth, over the eyes, and on the cheeks. Among other functions, they help rabbits orient themselves in underground warrens.

Claws

For wild rabbits, **digging tunnels** is a survival strategy. The claws serve as tools, and as a result they must keep growing back to remain usable.

Teeth

A RABBIT'S TEETH GROW 4 INCHES (10 CM) PER YEAR and get worn down only through intensive gnawing and chewing. Rabbits always need something to gnaw.

Ears

Built in the **SHAPE OF A FUN-NEL**, the ears can turn independently of each other. Without moving its head, a rabbit has a field of hearing of about 360 degrees. Its hearing is fine, and the animal reacts quite sensitively to all loud noises. Rabbits panic easily, especially when the noises happen suddenly, are unfamiliar, and are shrill (like the cry of a bird of prey). Continuous noise in their environment causes stress in the animals.

Tongue

The taste buds are **INSIDE THE RABBIT'S MOUTH** and throat. A rabbit can distinguish sweet, sour, bitter, and salty. Juicy greens and aromatic hay are particularly tasty.

Stamping, also known as thumping: When the rabbit pounds the ground with its hind feet, it means, "Watch out! There's danger nearby! I am afraid." This is how wild rabbits warn one another of approaching enemies.

Jumping into the air and flicking the heels together: This is one way in which wild rabbits try to get away from their enemies. If rabbits are allowed to romp around free as house pets, they use this to keep fit.

Lying flat on the ground with ears laid back, eyes anxiously dilated: Something has frightened your rabbit badly. Remain calm and under no circumstances run toward the rabbit.

Relaxed crouch, ears laid back: "If there's nothing wrong, I can munch and doze for hours."

Reclining on one side with legs stretched out, head on the ground: "I'm exhausted from romping around. Now I need some recovery time and I don't want to be disturbed."

Tense posture with front part of body and head stretched forward: "I'm on the lookout and ready to flee or to attack."

Three very different young rabbits: on the left, Pumpernickel, a red dwarf; center, Whiskers, a young lion-headed dwarf ram; and finally the German Giant mix named Max.

In addition, with ears slightly forward, tail tucked in: "I'll approach out of curiosity, but I don't feel secure with unfamiliar things."

Same posture, but with tail held stiffly erect: "Let's see who that is. I'm curious, but I'm not afraid."

Front part of body and head likewise extended and ready to leap, scut (tail) held high, but ears laid back, possibly brief purring: "Don't get too close or I will scratch and bite you."

Shaking the ears: This behavior is also frequently observed in dwarf rabbits. Generally it's the equivalent of "I don't like this at all."

Digging with the forepaws while on your lap may mean, "Keep petting me." But sexually mature bucks and females that are in heat or pregnant often dig restlessly in their bedding.

Pinching and nudging in rabbit society is usually not serious bickering (in contrast to serious biting). If a dwarf pinches you, don't yell "ouch," but rather put the rabbit down and leave it alone.

Marking: Does your dwarf rub its chin on objects? That's how it marks its territory. "All this belongs to me. This is my house." Droppings and urine are likewise marked individually with the help of scent glands. This marking behavior can lead to housebreaking problems later on.

It Makes Sense to Help

TIPS FROM THE
RABBIT EXPERT
Monika Wegler

EMERGENCIES In animal shelters and private animal protection organizations there are thousands of rabbits waiting for good homes. Just take a look, and don't worry: Not all rabbits in shelters have been traumatized by their unfortunate fate. Many were simply discarded; they are loving, friendly, and well suited even to beginners with rabbits.

ADVANTAGES Rabbits from an animal shelter have been checked by a veterinarian, and the bucks have already been neutered. If you choose an adult rabbit, it's much easier to check out their nature and appearance. This is not so easy with the little ones.

BY THE PAIR If you choose two that are already friends, there will be no difficulties with socialization.

RESPONSIBILITY A contract from the shelter and a check of the premises serve the welfare of the animals and are a component of serious animal welfare work. Your donation also makes it possible to help other rabbits.

Who's Right for Whom?

At around eight weeks, baby rabbits are ready for a new home. Young rabbits, especially littermates up to the age of about three months, can be kept in the same cage right from the beginning. Older dwarf rabbits that either don't know each other or join a rabbit you already own must first get used to one another (see p. 52).

A pair consisting of a doe and a buck is the ideal combination, and they almost always get along. But be careful: Between the third and fourth months of life rabbits reach sexual maturity. Promptly introduce the buck to the veterinarian, who can set a date for neutering the male, depending on the animal's development.

Two bucks: As youngsters two bucks can live harmoniously together. But with increasing sexual maturity, they begin to fight violently over territory and hierarchy. You have to control this behavior, which is totally natural for rabbits, through early neutering. Two potent rams together in one cage amounts to animal abuse and can end in death. With early neutering, there is no further obstacle to a peaceful life together.

Two does: While they are in heat, two does sometimes tend to defend their territory against their rival. If a neutered buck is added to the mix, the relationship goes more smoothly. But in the case of continual heat and false pregnancy, spaying is advisable for health reasons.

Small group: If you have enough space, you can also keep two pairs together, or combine two females with a neutered buck, or vice versa.

Safe transport: This box is great for trips to the veterinarian or as temporary accommodations while you clean the cage.

Buyer Beware

HEALTH Look for shiny fur with no bald spots. The eyes must be clear, the ears free from any type of coating; the nose must be dry, the anus clean. Hands off if an animal continually shows disease symptoms (danger of infection).

FRIENDLINESS This depends on the parent animals' disposition and on loving attention. See for yourself by visiting the breeder on-site, or ask at the pet shop where the animals come from. Rabbits from "reproduction mills" often remain shy.

GOOD LIVING CONDITIONS Cleanliness, plenty of space, healthy food, and competent advice make for a good report card.

A Little Information About Dwarf Rabbit Breeds

A variety of animals are offered for sale on the market and from private individuals under the designation of *dwarf rabbits*. When the animals are young, the mixed breeds are at first just as small as thoroughbred dwarfs. But what can you do if the presumed dwarf grows into a considerably larger, 9-pound (4-kilo) rabbit? Even though I personally am a fan of the "gentle giants," many homes are not ready for this type of "surprise" for reasons of space.

Purebred Dwarfs

On the following pages I will introduce you to several dwarf breeds. All the rabbits pictured there are prize-winning show animals that thoroughly meet the breed standards. This will give you a good idea of how "real" dwarfs look.

Standard: The standard codifies the guidelines according to which purebred animals are bred and evaluated by judges in shows. The standard is recognized by various rabbit breeding associations.

The dwarf type: A hereditary factor is responsible for the typical phenotype of a dwarf rabbit (designated by the letters *DW*). All dwarf rabbits carry it. Only the dwarf lops are lops that have been bred small.

The lion-headed rabbit is not a recognized breed, but it's highly esteemed among dwarf rabbit

owners. Two different examples of these dwarfs are pictured on pages 32 and 42.

Note: It's best to get purebred dwarfs straight from a registered association breeder. You will find addresses of associations that have Internet sites on page 62.

Picking up and carrying: The hands support the upper and lower body, with the dwarf rabbit's paws secured between the fingers.

Blue Eye

Polish

Weight and body: ideally, 2½ to 3 pounds (1.1 to 1.35 kg; 2¼ to 3⅓ pounds / 1.0 to 1.5 kg) possible. Short, cobby (stocky), cylindrical body the same width through front- and hindquarters, well-rounded hips. **Head** large in proportion to body, short with broad forehead and muzzle, broad nasal bone. **Ears:** standing close together, attractively rounded at the top, well haired. **Fur:** short, thick, soft; guard hairs: fine, even. **Coat color:** pure white in topcoat and undercolor. **Eye color:** with red-eyed albinos, transparent red; blue with blue eyes. **Claw color:** colorless.

Agouti (wild gray)

Netherland Dwarf

Weight, body, head, ears, coat: 2½ to 3 pounds (1.1 to 1.35 kg) ideal (from 2 to 3⅓ pounds [1.0–1.5 kg]). Short, compact, rounded, equally wide from front to back, hindquarters well rounded. **Coat color:** variations are wild gray, marten, dark gray, steel gray, and agouti. **Fur:** individual hairs have multiple bands of light and dark. With agouti: back with dark shading, chest and sides lighter, ears rimmed in black. Stomach, insides of legs, edge of chin and cheeks, and underside of tail are white. With agouti, reddish-brown, bluish undercolor. **Eye color:** dark brown. **Claw color:** dark horn colored.

Havana

Netherland Dwarf

Weight, body, head, ears, coat as in standard description for the Polish. **Coat color:** guard hairs rich, dark brown, with no gray streaking or white hairs; it extends over the entire body. The richer and shinier the brown, the better. Undercolor blue down to base of hairs. Visible only by blowing into fur or stroking against the lay of the hair. The fur color corresponds to the medium-sized Havana rabbit breed and the cat breed of the same name. **Eye color:** brown, slightly transparent red. **Claw color:** dark horn colored.

Chinchilla Colored
Netherland Dwarf

Weight, body, head, ears, fur as in standard description for the Polish. **Fur color:** guard hairs shiny bluish, light ash gray, produced by black and white guard hairs that project over the black long, coarse hairs. Edges of ears lined in black. White belly and underside of scut (tail). The young are born blue-black; the chinchilla color becomes visible only after around two weeks. The fur color corresponds to the larger chinchilla rabbit breed. **Eye color:** dark brown. **Claw color:** black-brown.

Black
Netherland Dwarf

Weight, body, head, ears, coat as in standard description for the Polish. **Coat color:** The guard hairs are dark black and shiny, with no red sheen or light spots. The undercolor is dark blue. The fur color corresponds to the medium-sized Black Vienna and Alaska rabbit breeds. This black Netherland Dwarf is a challenge for me as a photographer. This dwarf needs an extra-bright flash to show the beautiful blue sheen in the pitch-black fur. **Eye color:** dark brown. **Claw color:** black-brown to black.

Himalaya Colored, Black and White
Netherland Dwarf

Weight, body, head, ears, coat as in standard description for the Polish. **Markings:** snow white with black mask (which should cover only the nose), black ears, and black "booties." The scut has a pure, rich color. The markings are purest in the winter (cold-darkening). With the blue and white Himalaya-colored Netherland Dwarf the blue markings are on a white primary color. The markings correspond to the small Russian rabbit breed. **Eye color:** shiny red as with albinos. **Claw color:** dark brown.

White (Black) Ticked, Silver Marten Colored
Netherland Dwarf

Weight, body, head, ears, coat as in standard description for the Polish. **Markings:** Primary color is black, blue, or brown, depending on color variety. It is distributed over the entire body and is interspersed with longer, white-tipped hairs. Stomach, inside of legs, underside of scut, eye rings, edge of chin and cheeks, nostrils, and ears are always white. The markings correspond to the medium-sized Silver Marten rabbit breed. **Eye color:** dark brown, blue-gray only with blue animals. **Claw color:** dark.

Thuringer Colored
Netherland Dwarf

Weight, body, head, ears, coat as in standard description for the Polish. **Markings:** a reddish-yellow brown body color with darker hairs that lie over it evenly like a sooty haze (chamois colored). Mask, ears, and legs are dark like soot, but the transitions in the markings are gradual. On the sides and hindquarters of this dwarf rabbit there is a broad, sooty stripe. The markings correspond to the medium-sized Thuringer rabbit breed. **Eye color:** brown. **Claw color:** dark horn colored.

Havana Colored
Fox Dwarf

Weight, body, head, and ears as with the Polish and the Netherland Dwarfs. **Coat:** The Fox Dwarf rabbit's fur is 2–2½ inches (5–6 cm) long, with shorter fur on the head, ears, and legs. This dwarf has a thick undercoat, which is nonetheless supported by lots of long, coarse hairs. As a result, the fur does not tend to become matted as it does with other long-haired dwarfs. **Coat color:** white or Havana colored. **Eye color:** brown; red or blue in white animals. **Claw color:** dark; colorless in white animals.

Red
Rex Dwarf

Weight, body, head, and ears as with the Polish or Netherland Dwarfs. **Fur:** With this short-haired breed, the individual hairs stand at right angles to the skin. They should not be curled, and should be only ½ inch to slightly over ⅝ inch (14–17 mm) long. When you stroke against the lay of the fur, the hairs should remain erect and return to position slowly. **Fur, eye, and claw color:** Similar to the recognized larger Rex rabbit, such as the self-colored (single-colored) Rex, the checkered Rex, and the best known, the Beaver Rex.

Siam Yellow
Dwarf Lop

Weight: 3 to 4½ pounds (1.4–2 kg). **Body:** Short, cobby, broad shouldered, well muscled. **Head:** curved nose line (ram's nose), broad forehead and muzzle. **Ears:** horseshoe shaped; bulges (known as crown) at base of ears. Ear length: 9½ to 11 inches (24–28 cm). **Fur:** medium long with ample coarse hairs. **Fur, eye, and claw color:** corresponds to the recognized color variety. Siam Yellow: crème primary color with dark mask and scut, plus dark ears and legs. Stripes on back, shading on rump and shoulder.

Checkered (Gray-White)
Dwarf Lop

Weight, body, head, ears, and coat as in the standard description of the Siam Yellow above. So-called mini-lops are bred in Holland and England; they are lighter (no heavier than 3½ pounds / 1.6 kg) and have shorter ears (8¼ to 10 inches / 21–26 cm long). **Coat color:** white chest, legs, and stomach, likewise the lower jaw and edge of jaw and cheeks. A white spot in the center of the forehead. Head, crown, ears, and rump are covered by the gray markings. There are also lops in other colors. **Eye color:** dark brown. **Claw color:** colorless (white).

A Comfortable Home

As house pets our dwarf rabbits are forced to live differently from their wild counterparts. And yet even inside the house it is possible to offer the lively little creatures an environment that provides lots of variety and adequate exercise.

How Nice It Can Be at Home

A large outdoor enclosure in the yard with some furnishings is, of course, a dream come true for rabbits. But even we humans don't all live in a villa with our own park. It doesn't matter, for my suggestions for living conditions for dwarf rabbits are feasible even in limited space and will afford the animals an existence worth living.

The Ideal Indoor Cage

Pet shops sell various cage models that generally consist of a plastic lower shell and a removable mesh upper part.

Cage Size: The minimum floor area for two dwarfs should be 24 × 48 inches (120 × 60 cm). A spacious cage measuring around 32 × 57 inches (145 cm × 80 cm) is comfortable. If you don't have much space but still want to give your rabbits more room for exercise, I suggest a multiple-story home (see p. 62).

Bottom Pan: A pan height of 6 to 7 inches (16–18 cm) is perfectly adequate to keep the rabbits from digging the bedding out of the cage. Bottom pans that are too high simply keep the rabbits from seeing out. And what creature wants to stare at a plastic wall day in and day out?

Mesh Top: The top should have horizontal bars on which the animals can stretch and support themselves. Since rabbits occasionally gnaw on the mesh, galvanized tops are preferable to ones that are coated with plastic. A hinged flap on the front allows the dwarfs to hop in and out on their own. If there are two doors in the cage roof, you can easily tinker inside the cage. The cage height should be at least 18 inches (45 cm), so that the dwarfs can hunker down on the roof of their house.

Note: I advise against plastic hoods because they don't let in enough fresh air.

The Basics in a Rabbit House

Every indoor cage requires a certain amount of basic equipment, plus some small additions to help keep the rabbit occupied. But be careful you don't put too much "furniture" into the cage. Otherwise it will become too crowded and the rabbits won't be able to get enough exercise in the cage.

Practical Advice on Bedding

I recommend the following bedding mixture, which has proven its merits in my several decades of experience, and which my rabbits still prefer. On the bottom of the cage goes a layer of small-animal litter made from untreated softwood shavings about 2 to 3 inches (5–7 cm) deep, to soak up the urine. Over that I put a thick layer of straw (oat or wheat straw), in which the little creatures like to snuggle. In addition to hay, many rabbits really like to nibble straw.

Pellets made from pressed straw, corn, wood, or hemp are also a type of dust-free, absorbent bedding for small animals. However, it takes some time for the hard pellets to get trampled into a soft mat by the animals. Until that time the animals have to crouch on the hard chunks, which offer them scant comfort.

Why a Hayrack Is a Good Idea

Hay is the rabbit's "daily bread" and is best presented in a rack. If you simply lay the hay onto the floor and the dwarfs don't eat up their ration right away, it too quickly becomes soiled. I recommend a plastic hayrack that attaches to the bars from the outside and thus saves space in the cage (see photo at right).

There is a risk of injury with hayracks made of wire that you hang inside the cage. Young rabbits especially like to jump inside, and they can get their legs hung up in the mesh and hurt themselves seriously. Cover the top of such hayracks with a board.

Pros and Cons of Water Dispensers

Rabbits must always have plenty of clean, fresh water available.

> Water dispensers with a ball valve protect the water from contamination, but if the dispensing head is not cleaned thoroughly, germs can take up residence. In addition, drinking from a dispenser requires an unnatural crick in the animal's neck.

> If you offer the water in a heavy stoneware bowl, the rabbits are much happier to drink from it, for it matches their natural drinking behavior. But unfortunately, bedding gets into the water all too quickly. My recommendation: Place the bowl off the floor and on a cinder block.

No Plastic in the Cage

PLASTIC ITEMS do not belong in a rabbit's home. If the animals gnaw on it, they can develop serious health problems.

THE NEED TO GNAW Hang twigs to gnaw in the ceiling mesh, or attach an untreated board for gnawing on the side of the cage.

ATMOSPHERE The hayrack hangs on the bars of the cage from the outside, and thus takes up no room inside the cage. The stable food dish is raised on a cinder block with rounded edges; it is impregnated with an organic pigment for better cleaning. The "scratching pyramid" next to the food dish is a new item from the pet shop. It consists of pressed mineral earth and herbs—scratching and nibbling fun all rolled into one. Clean water dispensers thoroughly!

WORKING FOR FOOD This food ball contains healthy treats, banishes boredom, and contributes to fitness. Hang the ball from the center of the cage roof. This allows your dwarf to develop its sense of balance more effectively. You can very easily put together your own food chain like the one in the photo on page 34. It not only looks nice, but also provides exercise, a way to pass the time, and pleasure for the palate.

HELP GOING IN AND OUT The flexible bridge made from natural wood helps the rabbit get into and out of the cage without risk. That way the dwarf can't get its legs stuck in the bars of the door.

Food Dishes

Use only heavy, glazed stoneware dishes, preferably with a rim that turns inward to keep the rabbit from digging the food out so easily. Plastic dishes will get gnawed, and they tip over easily. Use smaller dishes with young dwarfs, for they like to crouch right in the middle of the food. Otherwise I use dishes with a diameter of around 6 inches (15 cm).

A Little House for Snuggling

Rabbits need a little house into which they can retreat and feel protected. Whether you buy or make the house, pay particular attention to the following:
> Only wood houses are suitable for rabbits.
> A flat roof offers the dwarf an additional elevated resting place.
> Young dwarfs are still growing. It's better to choose a larger model, because otherwise it will be too small later on.
> Sometimes dwarfs fight inside the hutch. If one of the animals flees into the little house and gets cornered by the "attacker," a second emergency exit will keep the fight from escalating.

A Toilet in the Indoor Cage

Rabbits generally search out a special place to leave their droppings. You can place a plastic bowl filled with absorbent straw pellets in that place. A corner toilet with a plastic hood saves a lot of space. If you are lucky, your dwarfs will use this toilet and not gnaw on it. I prefer to clean the "corner" daily. Try it for yourself.
Warning: Cat litter is absolutely taboo! If a rabbit eats it, it clogs the digestive tract and the animal can die.

The rabbit can dig to its heart's content in a natural wood box filled with sand. Coat the bottom and inner walls with clear lacquer.

The **Right Location** Is Important

A COMFORTABLE TEMPERATURE Rabbits are sensitive to heat and prefer cool temperatures. In the winter the cage should not be placed near the radiator, and in the summer, avoid glaring sunlight. An ideal temperature is about 65°F (18°C), give or take a couple of degrees.

QUIET SURROUNDINGS Dwarf rabbits have a much finer sense of hearing than we people do. Keep music soft, and avoid loud yelling. Also a location that people are continually walking by causes stress and disturbs dwarf rabbits tremendously.

DRAFT This is often a danger at floor level. Rabbits don't tolerate draft and catch cold quickly. Place the cage on something like a discarded child's mattress (approx. 4.5 × 2.5 feet / 1.4 × 0.7 m).

Out of the Cage and Bound for Adventure!

Keeping rabbits in a cage all the time is agony for these active animals. If they can hop around free in the house, they are exposed to all kinds of dangers. On pages 24 and 25 I propose an indoor enclosure that measures 18 square feet (5.4 sq. m), which can be connected directly to the indoor cage (multistory house). Here the little rascals are surely in good hands and can dig, hide, jump, and gnaw to their heart's content. My experience-proven furnishings can be bought at a pet shop or a building supplies store, or with a little skill you can make them yourself.

The Floor of the Enclosure: Smooth surfaces are easy to clean, but because of the danger of slipping, they are totally inappropriate for the active hoppers. A tile floor is too cold, and wood and carpeted floors are hard to keep clean—especially in the presence of urine. So I recommend the following combination, which has worked out the best with my rabbits: Place a waterproof tarp on the existing floor. Put a thick layer of newspapers over this to soak up any urine that may seep through. The "rabbit meadow" consists of a chewable rice or corn straw mat (available at a reasonable cost in building supplies stores). But if your dwarfs are little "pigpens" that leave lakes of urine in addition to the droppings that are easy to vacuum up, the topmost layer should be a durable, easy-to-clean overlay of carpet (see photo,

pp. 24–25). Pull the outer edges of the overlay outside the fencing for the enclosure where the rabbits' teeth can't reach them.

Note: Loose runners, individual tiles, and carpets with loops of thread are inappropriate. See page 26.

This clay pot full of nibbling treats is rich in vitamins: On top is *Callisia repens* (a food plant), with kitchen herbs and grasses on the side. The little bunnies find it delicious.

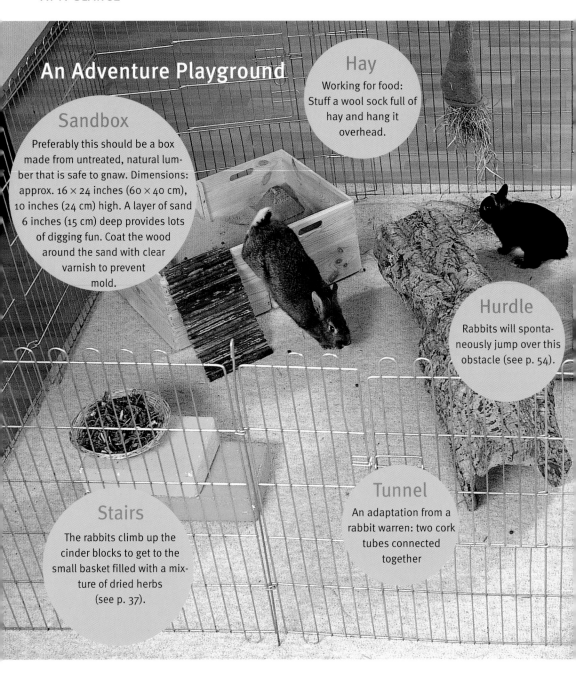

An Adventure Playground

Hay

Working for food: Stuff a wool sock full of hay and hang it overhead.

Sandbox

Preferably this should be a box made from untreated, natural lumber that is safe to gnaw. Dimensions: approx. 16 × 24 inches (60 × 40 cm), 10 inches (24 cm) high. A layer of sand 6 inches (15 cm) deep provides lots of digging fun. Coat the wood around the sand with clear varnish to prevent mold.

Hurdle

Rabbits will spontaneously jump over this obstacle (see p. 54).

Stairs

The rabbits climb up the cinder blocks to get to the small basket filled with a mixture of dried herbs (see p. 37).

Tunnel

An adaptation from a rabbit warren: two cork tubes connected together

Tree

A place to stretch and reach for treats

Leaf Basket

A grazing basket with dried autumn leaves: Rabbits love to rustle around inside. The rabbits like to eat the dried leaves, which are a healthy source of roughage.

Tower

The stackable natural wood boxes from a building supplies store are turned into a tower. Filled with straw, they make a place for cuddling and hiding.

Bridge

The rabbit gets a treat by going over the bridge and the little hut with a ramp: a bowl with fresh grass and herbs. If the little scamp polishes everything off, replant the bowl. This is a great vitamin cocktail in the winter.

Fencing: For security I have two outdoor rabbit enclosures from the pet shop; the individual sections are connected but still move freely. They make it possible to set up the adventure playground according to your living conditions and still expand or move the enclosure. Two elevated doors (one per enclosure) facilitate ease of entry but keep the dwarfs from getting out. The sections of wire fencing are 32 inches (80 cm) high and adequate for an indoor enclosure.

Free Access: The door to the rabbit house always opens into the enclosed run and is kept open. That way the dwarf rabbits can decide for themselves where they want to linger. This is, after all, the purpose of this enclosure: to provide more round-the-clock free exercise and activity to the indoor rabbits in a protected environment—even without your supervision.

Additional Security: Put a cage that sits on the floor against the wall of the room and situate all elevated sitting places far enough away from the fencing; otherwise the sly dwarfs will use everything as a springboard out of their enclosure. You must attach a board to the top of a low cage for protection. That way when a dwarf jumps on and off it won't get caught and injure itself (this also makes a great lookout point). Baby dwarf rabbits are small, but they are great at discovering the tiniest crawl spaces. One special favorite is the free space between the wire sections and the bottom pan of the cage, which tapers toward the bottom. I block off these empty spots with stones or boards.

Rabbits Need Exercise

If rabbits get little or no exercise and activity, their life expectancy is reduced. The rabbits then tend to gain weight, their muscles atrophy, and their circulatory system grows weaker. A joyless existence in a cage has an effect on our little guests' quality of life. Without stimulation and exercise, dwarf rabbits become either apathetic or aggressive. That's why I recommend my indoor enclosure.

A movable enclosure made from sections of wire and containing places to creep into is good for hours in the yard.

This airy shelter made from a trellis of willow offers protection from the sun and gnawing enjoyment. My dwarf rabbits love it.

The flexible string of wood stakes cut in half (edging for a flower bed, available in garden shops) is great for creating a natural space divider.

Excursions in the Yard

Hopping around on a lawn, chewing grass stems, and sniffing the wonderful scents in nature make a rabbit's heart beat faster. But here too you are responsible for the rabbit's safety. Just letting the rabbits run around in the yard is no more appropriate than walking them on a leash in the park.

Setting Up a Movable Enclosure

The fencing for the enclosure can be set up in the yard in a few minutes using sections of wire (see photo, p. 26). The adventure playground (see photo pp. 24–25) and balcony run are likewise fenced in (see photo, p. 28).

Size: If you combine two enclosures, the rabbits get a run of around 15 to 30 square feet (3–10 sq. m). The dwarfs can romp to their hearts' content.

Keeping Watch: Keep the dwarfs in sight. It's best to put the creatures into the enclosure when you are also in the yard. With no supervision for hours, many a dwarf has dug an escape tunnel under the wire fence. The net that comes with the fencing is intended to protect the enclosure from above, such as from birds of prey. I do without it, though, because in the past high-jumping rabbits have become tangled in the net. Smaller enclosures can be covered with wire mesh stretched over a wooden frame.

Health Protection: To keep the grass fresh for chewing and clean, the pen must be relocated regularly. Otherwise the droppings will attract dangerous maggots (see p. 45). Also, any use of herbicides and pesticides constitutes a danger to the animals' health.

Climate Change: Put indoor rabbits outdoors only when springtime temperatures have moderated (65°F / 18°C, plus or minus 4 degrees).

Beware of Heatstroke! Rabbits can tolerate neither intense sunlight nor excessive heat. A folding pavilion with no walls provides air and shade, even in the hot summer. If you use a tree for shade, don't forget to take into account the movement of the sun.

Setup: An empty pen without shelter set up on the lawn is not only boring for rabbits, but also it causes anxiety in the animals. In the photos on pages 26 and 27 I provide some suggestions for how to set up a pen. All the items are made from totally harmless, natural materials, and the hiding places also provide the dwarf rabbits with a well-ventilated, shady spot even in the summer (see also p. 56).

› The hollow log is one that I found in the woods. This is a tree trunk from which the soft, rotten insides were carefully scraped out.

› A terra cotta flowerpot with a broken bottom was padded with straw and adapted into a cuddling place near the hollow log. Stones placed at the sides keep it from rolling.

› I constructed the sturdy little house in the foreground from four old roofing tiles.

› An armful of reeds tied together and placed over the wooden house and the willow trellis provides some activity for the rabbits.

› The tent made from two woven willow trellises is a hit with my rabbits.

› You can set up a run in the yard with edging for a flower bed (a flexible chain made from wooden dowels cut in half lengthwise).

› Twigs with leaves (hornbeam in this instance) are tied together at the top and placed over a perch. This is a great place to cuddle that can be nibbled to heart's content.

› A little basket full of hay and a full water bowl always belong in the run.

Note: If you want to keep your rabbits outdoors for an extended time, you have to build them a sturdy pen that's completely secure against entry and exit. (Directions are in my large handbook *My Dwarf Rabbits* [see Books, p. 62]).

This balcony run with a hutch provides lots of variety and a great fresh-air oasis for two dwarf rabbits.

Small Balconies

As an alternative or a complement to indoor living, you can set up a home for your dwarf rabbits on the balcony.

Security: Wherever there are small openings in the railing, they must be closed. A good choice for this is galvanized rabbit fencing—.039 inch (1 mm) thick, with a mesh size of .660 or 1 inch (17 or 25 mm)—which can stand up to rabbit teeth. A ground-level balcony must also be secured overhead against possible intrusion from predators or cats.

Sunshade: Rabbits are very sensitive to heat and absolutely need well-ventilated, shady spots. An awning or large umbrella is useful. Always keep an eye on the changes in the position of the sun.

Floor: Balconies with a concrete floor or tiles are slippery and too cold. I recommend a natural rice or corn straw mat for the covered floor protected from rain. Or else you can build an enclosure into which you put small-animal or cattle bedding. I advise against the indoor-outdoor carpeting that is sometimes recommended. It's made of nothing but plastic, is hard to clean, and is much too prickly for rabbits. A discarded cotton throw rug is a better choice for the summer (see photo, p. 28).

Climate Change: Put indoor rabbits outside only when the springtime temperatures moderate (65°F / 18°C, give or take 4 degrees). In the cold weather, rabbits that live outdoors must not be brought indoors quickly to "warm up." A change in the other direction is positively dangerous to the rabbits' health.

Long-term Accommodations: The dwarfs need a well-insulated, winter-proof hutch filled with plenty of straw.

The Proper **Balcony**

TIPS FROM THE RABBIT EXPERT
Monika Wegler

DIRECTION If your balcony faces the east, southeast, or southwest, this is ideal. Balconies facing directly south get too hot in the summer. And yet on the side exposed to the weather it's almost always too damp and much too drafty.

ROOFING If there is another balcony right above yours, it will provide protection from above. Otherwise at least the part where the hutch or the little house stands must be provided with a weatherproof roof.

RAILING The railing should be as high and as solid as possible so that you have less work to do in making it secure (see text at left).

SIZE A run of 20 square feet (6 sq. m) is advisable for two rabbits. A very large balcony can be divided with fencing so it can be used by both humans and animals (see photo, p. 28).

GROUND LEVEL It's ideal when trees shade a large part of the balcony. Otherwise you will have to provide well-ventilated, shady places.

Healthy Nutrition

A rabbit's digestive system is adapted to plant foods that are poor in nutrients and rich in roughage. Feed your rabbits this type of diet. That way you will avoid digestive problems and help keep the animals healthy and fit.

The Right Way to Feed Your Dwarf Rabbits

If we don't eat healthy foods, in the short or the long run we get sick. It's the same with rabbits. It is neither complicated nor costly to feed your dwarf rabbits properly. For example, you can collect food plants when you take a walk. The exercise and the fresh air will also be good for your health. And when you eat fresh fruit and vegetables every day during the winter, you can buy fresh produce for the rabbits at the same time. That's the way I do it.

The Staple Food: Hay

Hay must always be part of healthy nutrition for rabbits. It must be available to your dwarfs around the clock. There is no substitute for hay, and it should make up around 70 percent of the food. But why is hay so important?

› The high-fiber roughage keeps the digestion working. It assures a smooth passage through the intestines.

› Hay balances out the fermentation process and thus encourages healthy intestinal flora.
› It helps prevent dangerous hair obstruction in the digestive tract (particularly important with all long-haired rabbits).
› The rabbits' teeth, which grow continuously, are worn down naturally by intensively chewing the hay stalks.
› Hay is not fattening. It is an ideal diet food for overweight rabbits, and for stomach and intestinal problems.
› And when things get boring, hay provides healthy chewing activity.

How to Tell if Hay Is Good

Good hay contains a variety of grasses, flower, and weeds. High-grade hay has a greenish color and gives off a pleasant scent. I recommend buying organic and alpine meadow hay (which also is good for the environment).

Unsuitable: Dusty, old, woody, damp, and moldy hay.

For Fussy Eaters: If you notice that your dwarfs eat little or no hay, put off feeding them the juicy morning greens for three to four hours. Instead, give the rabbits two big handfuls of tasty hay right in front of the hayrack in the hutch. You'll see how your "fussy eaters" turn into "hay freaks" and hungrily clean up their portion.

Hay Allergy: If a veterinarian identifies a hay allergy in your rabbit, you should not switch to compressed hay, for this is not an equivalent substitute for natural hay. My recommendation: Dip the hay in a bucket with clear tap water and "wash" it thoroughly. Then shake the entire contents in a colander or strainer; wring the wet hay out thoroughly, and poor the "broth" down the drain. Now you can feed your dwarf the washed hay in the hayrack or in a separate food dish. But make sure that the damp serving of hay—offered fresh every day—gets eaten. It must not be left lying around to encourage the growth of mold.

Do Rabbits Also Need to Drink?

The clear answer is "yes." Every rabbit needs fresh, clean drinking water every day. Many rabbits drink a lot, and others only a little—leave that up to your rabbits. At midday check to see if the water bottle or bowl is at least half full of water; if it's not, fill it up again. If your tap water contains lots of chlorine, boil it first, let it cool off, and serve it cool. If the water contains lots of nitrates, it's healthier for your rabbit to drink noncarbonated mineral water.

Notice: Milk is off-limits to rabbits. A rabbit that gets a healthy diet will also not need supplementary vitamin drops. Thinned chamomile tea is used only for therapeutic purposes.

Choco, a lion-headed dwarf rabbit, really likes the taste of yarrow.

Fresh Food from Nature

As soon as the first green stalks sprout in the fields, I reduce my rabbits' winter feeding of vegetables and fruit. From now until the fall I pluck the treats that nature offers in the surrounding pastures: grasses, flowers, wild plants, and herbs. Even if you live in a large city, as I do, if you need merely look around to find some fields where you can pluck the rabbits' favorite foods.

Recommended Gathering Places: Undeveloped, overgrown plots of land are ideal, as are fallow fields, such as road embankments or old cemeteries. Often there are meadows in large parks off the customary "dog walking routes," in fenced playgrounds that dogs can't get into. If you have a yard, it's a good idea to set aside an area and put in a meadow of appropriate flowers. You can get special seeds in gardening centers. Otherwise you can find great, natural meadows in all types of terrain.

Inappropriate Areas: Do not collect greens from the edge of traveled roads (contamination from auto exhaust) or from fields where dogs have access (danger of illness through droppings and urine).

A Mixture Is Best

If you watch wild rabbits graze, you see that they munch a little here and a little there. They never eat just one food plant. In accordance with this natural eating behavior I give my rabbits a good mixture of greens from outdoors. In my decades of experience, this is best for the animals.

Recommended Greens and Succulent Foods Year-Round

FOOD PLANTS YOU CAN GATHER		FROM KITCHEN AND GARDEN	
WILD PLANTS	all grasses, dandelion, field bindweed, plantain, coltsfoot, common orache, goosefoot, chickweed, common vetch, white clover, alfalfa, wild strawberry, daisy	VEGETABLES	Carrots and tops, fennel, wild celery, celery, broccoli, cucumber, squash, zucchini, parsnips, turnips, organic lettuce. In winter: lamb's lettuce and lettuce. Only a little Chinese cabbage and kohlrabi leaves. Stay away from all other types of cabbage (very gassy)
MEDICINAL HERBS	calendula, chamomile, wild sage, yarrow		
FOOD FOR NIBBLING	lots of twigs, buds, leaves from hazelnut, hornbeam, malaceous fruits (apples and pears). Small quantities: maple, birch, alder, linden, poplar, willow, fir, fig	HERBS:	calendula, chamomile, wild sage, yarrow
		FRUIT:	apple, pear, strawberry, raspberry

DO NOT FEED: any twigs from stone fruits, oak, chestnut (yew and thuja are poisonous), any bulb plants, leek, legumes, eggplant, avocado, rhubarb. Note that raw potatoes and cabbage, green tomatoes, tomato leaves, and red beans are poisonous.

My Little Wild Mixture: These are easy to find in common fields with a limited number of plant species, even by people who aren't botanists: all types of grasses, long and short, plus dandelion (preferably the young leaves), a little clover, daisy, and if you can find and recognize them, plantain and yarrow (see Table: Recommended Greens and Succulent Foods, p. 33).

Gradual Changeover and Quantity: My rabbits get succulent and green foods all year long (one handful morning and evening for each dwarf). My youngest rabbits are also brought up that way, as the photos clearly show. But if your dwarfs are not used to this food, you have to introduce them to it carefully, "leaf by leaf" over a three-week period. Otherwise the dwarfs will pounce greedily onto the fresh greens, eat too much at once, and develop severe digestive problems. No rabbit can withstand such a radical change of food. More on this topic is in the rules for feeding (see p. 35).

If you have to work for your treats, you don't get bored. I threaded these healthy snacks on a string and hung them up high enough so that the dwarfs have to stretch to reach them.

Fresh Vitamins All Year Long

For wild rabbits the winter months are a time of great privation. The animals have to dig through the layer of snow to get to roots and moss and satisfy their hunger. Many are also hungry enough to gnaw tree bark, which displeases gardeners. Our pet rabbits have it easier. We can supply them year-round with green and succulent foods, herbs, and fruit (see Table, p. 33). These fresh, natural vitamins and nutrients keep the dwarf rabbits fit and healthy. Dry food with added "artificial" vitamins is no worthy substitute.

You can give your dwarf rabbits a carrot or an apple in their dish to supply them with vitamins. But I prefer to give my little gourmets a tasty dish of fruits and vegetables (see top photo, p. 21). That way my dwarf rabbits always get a variety of food, mixed and in small portions. As with green foods, this variety is good for the animals (see p. 33). On the other hand, if you give your dwarf rabbits too much of one type of food at one time, it may cause gas and diarrhea.

Winter Mix: Here's an example of how I feed my rabbits in the winter. Of course you can vary the combinations at will.

Here's the portion I figure for one meal for each dwarf rabbit:

$\frac{1}{4}$ apple or pear (remove seeds), one small carrot (sliced lengthwise), three finger-thick slices of wild celery, plus a handful of green food (such as parsley, carrot greens, or lamb's lettuce).

Proper Feeding made easy

TIPS FROM THE
RABBIT EXPERT
Monika Wegler

HAY The animals must always have this food staple available in adequate quantities.

FRESH AND CLEAN Thoroughly wash fruit and vegetables and feed only while fresh. Remove leftovers from the cage no later than the following morning.

REGULAR FEEDING TIMES It's best to feed morning and evening. The animals will get used to it, and you will notice when an animal has no appetite (a possible symptom of illness).

CHANGE OF FOOD Never make abrupt changes in diet. It's better to change over gradually, over a three- or four-week period, exchanging portion for portion.

WEIGHT CHECK Occasional weighing makes it easier to recognize "heavyweights" and put them onto a diet (hay and water and lots of exercise).

POSITIVELY HARMFUL Feed no food that is frozen, spoiled, moldy, or tainted with harmful substances. Leftovers from the table, cookies, and chocolate are also taboo.

About Food and Feeding

Proper nutrition is the best health maintenance program for your dwarf rabbits. Such animals "gleam" with beautiful fur, are lively, and have no problems with their figure as long as they also get enough exercise.

Good Choice

(+) Offer small treats, such as a piece of carrot, with your hand. This encourages trust.

(+) Let your dwarfs work for a portion of their food. This is good for their figure and prevents boredom.

(+) In the winter grow fresh food in a ceramic bowl on the windowsill. Use potting soil and seeds (such as grains, alfalfa, chervil). Also see p. 23.

(+) Healthy between-meals snacks for the dwarfs include slices of carrots or dried apple slices (untreated) from the pet shop.

Better Not

(–) Don't give food only inside the cage and in the dish. A dominant animal may defend it aggressively.

(–) Don't feed your dwarfs with inappropriate dry food. This could lead to digestive and tooth problems.

(–) Do not change foods abruptly! Dwarfs that previously have had no green food have to grow used to this food slowly; otherwise they may experience digestive problems.

(–) It's best not to feed the rabbits unknown plants. As you collect them, make sure that they are not poisonous to rabbits (see Internet addresses, p. 62).

What Kind of Dry Food Is Healthy?

If you feed your dwarf rabbits according to my recommendations, the animals will need no further commercial food. But if you prefer not to avoid such foods, you should observe the following:

› Be sure to look at the ingredients. The first ingredient is the one that's present in the greatest quantity.

› Grains, corn, nuts, sugar, and molasses are things that rabbits like to eat, but they don't agree with them. These ingredients can lead to serious digestive and tooth problems. Spare your dwarf rabbits the pain, and yourself the veterinarian bills.

› Don't be fooled by colorful packaging and rosy promises. A picture of happy rabbits on a flowery meadow doesn't mean that this food contains nothing but grasses, flower, and herbs.

› Not every red and green morsel in the food consists of dried vegetables.

› No such "health" dry food is appropriate as a single source of food for rabbits.

Healthy Dry Mixtures

These contain principally vegetables, herbs, and grasses. Here's about what the contents should be: fiber content at least 16 percent, fat content no higher than 2 to 3 percent, protein content no higher than 15 percent. Well-stocked pet shops sell healthy dry food mixtures for between-meals snacks. Ask for it; most shops respond to customers' desires.

Hands off granola bars, tastes of yogurt, and other exotic offerings. Chew stones are also unnecessary.

My young animals are raised with green foods right from the beginning. If your dwarf is not yet accustomed to it, the changeover must be gradual so that it doesn't produce serious digestive problems.

Care and Health

Rabbits are by nature clean creatures that regularly groom their fur. As owners our duty is to provide further care and preventive health measures. This involves a home that's always clean, where the dwarfs can feel their best.

Cleanliness Prevents Disease

No rabbit will feel comfortable in a home that is dirty and neglected. Damp, filthy bedding doesn't smell disagreeable only to us humans. These strong fumes also irritate the sensitive breathing apparatus of the dwarf rabbits. A neglected rabbit hutch is also the ideal breeding ground for various bacteria, and thus fosters disease.

Daily Cleaning Scrub out all food and water containers under hot water and dry thoroughly. Scrub out water bottles with a bottlebrush, and clean out the metal tube with a cotton swab. Use your hand to fluff up straw that has become trampled down so that droppings fall into the litter below. If the rabbits have left droppings in their sandbox, remove them with a slotted scoop (for cat litter boxes). Unfortunately this is not possible with toilets that use straw pellets. But I clean the "toilet corner" in the cage every day as a precautionary measure, especially in the summer. I also clean up the floor in the run (inside the house and on the balcony), since droppings left around can attract flies (see p. 45).

Thorough Weekly Cleaning Replace all the litter and bedding in the housing, litter boxes, and digging boxes with fresh. Scrub all trays and items such as wooden seats, hutch, and fixtures under hot water and dry thoroughly. Now you can put in fresh bedding.

Note: While you are doing the thorough cleaning, put the rabbits into a travel cage. There they can rest, and you don't continually need to keep an eye out for them. If you use cleaning agents, stick to ecologically sound ones. Disinfecting is necessary only in the case of contagious diseases (look for natural products).

The Care that Dwarf Rabbits Need

Even when they have good living conditions and healthy food, our little occupants feel better when we take regular care of them. This includes observing the rabbits closely on a daily basis. This is the only way to detect in a timely fashion when an animal suddenly acts differently from normal. This is the best way to recognize a developing illness early. And you should pick up every rabbit once a day and check it over thoroughly. I sit down in the run, take a dwarf onto my lap, and first pet it a lot. As I do so, I gently feel its body, stroke the fur

1 With this eight-week-old doe, the anal opening is easy to locate under the scut (tail), and the slit-shaped vagina is visible above it.

2 With a young buck look at the anal opening, and above it the dot-shaped sexual orifice. The little penis is hardly visible.

(including against the lay of the hairs), and take note of every conspicuous feature such as tiny wounds or lumps under the skin. Then I take the dwarf by the fur on the neck and turn it onto its back on my lap. Now I check the lower body, including the front and hind legs. I pay particular attention to the anal region, which must always be clean and free of droppings.

This daily health check is especially important with rabbits that are kept on a balcony or outdoors in the yard. It could even save your little friend's life (see p. 45).

Coat Care

Rabbits naturally change their coat in both the spring and the fall. This is most visible in animals that live outdoors all year long. With our indoor rabbits, the shedding is not so intense, but it takes place over a longer time.

Normal Length Hair Once a month, or weekly during shedding, brush the fur with a natural bristle brush in the direction of the hairs. Then remove any remaining loose hairs with a damp chamois cloth.

Long Hair The "fuzzies" really need lots of care. Unlike the long-haired Fox Dwarf (see p. 16), their fur doesn't have the supporting bristly hairs. As a result, their coat very easily becomes matted, and they depend on our regular care. The best way to work with the fur is to use special combs and brushes for Persian cats. Daily coat care will not be enough for Angora mixes. These animals must be shorn completely approximately on a quarterly basis.

Hair-ball Formation (Bezoars) If a rabbit swallows too many loose hairs as it licks its fur, they may clump together in a ball inside the digestive tract and cause serious digestive problems. Thus, regular combing and brushing is more than just beauty care.

Note: Don't put a rabbit into a bath or a shower! If necessary, carefully trim away smeared fur in the anal region. Soften any fecal remains in a chamomile soak, and then thoroughly dry the animal.

When the Claws Grow Too Long

Rabbits have claws that grow continuously and are useful in digging tunnels. But in indoor living, they don't use them often enough to wear them down. Thus, I check my rabbits' claws every two months and shorten them if necessary. Rabbits have five claws on their front paws, and four on the rear.

› The ideal length for the claws is slightly longer than the hair on the paws; the tips point toward the floor.

› If the claws grow too long, they turn inward like a sickle. This causes the toes to turn when the rabbit walks, and it becomes painful for the rabbit to run. Don't let things go this far.

› Clip the claws with a special claw cutter from the pet shop, about $\frac{1}{4}$ inch (7 mm) from the blood vessels (the living part). With light-colored claws, the living part is easy to see because of its reddish color.

› It's a good idea to illuminate dark claws with a strong flashlight from underneath.

3 Tooth check. This dwarf rabbit's teeth are the right length. The upper incisors should barely reach over the lower ones (scissor bite).

4 Cleaning up the genitals. These can harbor secretions that should be removed with a cotton swab dipped in baby oil.

5 Clipping the claws. A claw clipper must be used regularly to shorten the growing claws whenever they become too long (see text at left).

› Have your veterinarian or another expert show you how to trim the claws.

Note: If despite your best efforts you injure a blood vessel, press a clean handkerchief onto the wound for a minute and seal the location with a spray-on bandage.

Preventing Tooth Problems

A dwarf rabbit's teeth grow about 4 inches (10 cm) per year! They need some "chewing work" to wear them down naturally. Good tooth abrasion is fostered especially by green plants, hay, and twigs, plus natural wood; these also satisfy the innate need to chew.

Note: Rabbits can't grind up seeds and various types of pellets well enough with their molars; they can only squash them. The result can be serious tooth problems.

Checking the Teeth

With normal, healthy dentition, the front incisors in the upper jaw reach closely over the teeth in the lower jaw like scissors (scissors bite). I'm doing a tooth check in the photo on page 41. It shows a dwarf with the right length of teeth and the proper bite. Check your rabbit's teeth regularly.

Inborn Bite Deformities

Unfortunately, these occur too frequently, because careless breeders don't remove their genetically

Fuzzy sniffs the yarrow. With its fairly long fur, this lion-headed dwarf lop needs more coat care than a regular rabbit. I comb it out thoroughly every week.

impaired animals from breeding. That way the deformity is passed on, and not only with dwarfs, as often claimed, but also with larger rabbits. With a shortened upper jaw or a pincer bite there is an anomaly in the bite. The teeth can no longer wear away naturally, and they keep growing out of control. In the end the incisors in the upper jaw arc inward, and the ones on the lower jaw grow forward out of the mouth like elephant tusks. Don't wait for this to happen, for the afflicted rabbit must endure terrible discomfort, and can't even eat. Dwarf rabbits with an inborn bite deformity must have their teeth shortened by a veterinarian in a timely fashion and in rotation about every four weeks.

Note: Good veterinarians "trim" the incisors with a dental rotary file. If they are shortened with a clipper, there is a danger that the tooth will later split, with damage or destruction to the root.

Problems with the Molars

Laypeople can't check the deeper molars. But if you see that the hairs at the corners of the mouth are matted with saliva and the rabbit chews with nothing in its mouth, you must take it to a veterinarian. The reason may be the formation of points or hooks on the molars that interfere with the tongue or mucous membranes of the cheeks, causing severe inflammation.

Taking Care of Rabbits

TIPS FROM THE
RABBIT EXPERT
Monika Wegler

HOLD SECURELY While you are working with your rabbit, it may panic in an attempt to get free. To keep it from getting hurt, always hold the animal securely.

HAVE SOMEONE SHOW YOU THE HOLDS Are you uncertain, or do you have problems with the recommended holds? At first have a veterinarian or another expert (such as a breeder or pet shop owner) demonstrate them.

CLAW CARE You can put a natural slab of stone under the sand mixture in the digging box. When the dwarf digs, its claws will wear down naturally through contact with the rough surface.

INTIMATE CARE The groin glands are in skin pockets on both sides of the sex orifice. You can use a cotton swab dipped in baby oil to regularly remove built-up secretions from these places.

When a Dwarf Rabbit Becomes a Patient

Rabbits are hardy by nature. Oftentimes illnesses are caused by improper living conditions and poor nutrition. When a dwarf becomes sick or injured, it remains still and inconspicuous. This is an inborn protective behavior that keeps them from being noticed by predators. You have to observe and check over your little houseguests all the more thoroughly (see p. 40). The sooner you recognize an illness and treat it, the better the chances of recovery. Don't put off a visit to the veterinarian for too long. Many health problems that at first appear harmless can soon grow into acute, life-threatening diseases.

What to Watch For

Healthy dwarf rabbits hop around cheerfully, are alert to their environment, and eat with a healthy appetite. Their fur shines, their nose and eyes are free from any kind of discharge, the ears are clean, and the area below the muzzle is dry. The following changes are signs of disease symptoms that must be taken seriously.

> The dwarf merely crouches apathetically in a corner of the cage, or withdraws totally into its little house and refuses to come out.

> When you give the rabbit its daily food, the little one doesn't hop over to it with accustomed pleasure. It eats only very little or refuses to eat altogether.

> When the rabbit moves, it favors individual limbs, or it limps.

> Its stomach is distended and feels hard, and the rabbit's back is arched.

> The rabbit often holds its head at an angle, awkwardly turns in circles, and curls up.

> With severe pain, a rabbit gnashes its teeth.

> Its droppings are mushy and the anal region is smeared with droppings. Healthy rabbits leave well-formed, fairly dry, round droppings.

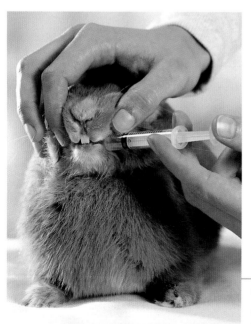

When administering liquid medications, use a disposable syringe (with no needle). Squirt the medicine into the side of the mouth.

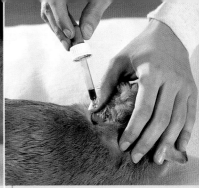

1 CAREFULLY dribble eye-drops onto the conjunctiva. Euphrasia (eyebright) from a health food store helps with such things as mild infections.

2 TAKE THE TEMPERATURE USING A LUBRICATED DIGITAL THER-MOMETER IN THE ANAL OPENING. The normal body temperature of a dwarf rabbit is 101–104°F (38.5–40°C).

3 SMALL INJURIES heal quickly if you dribble a little Swedish bitters onto them. It disinfects and is an antibiotic. If you can't find this in stores, order it from the Internet.

Cecum Excrement Occasionally you will find a discharge in the bedding; it consists of soft, shiny, moist pills that stick together like grapes. These are the remains of what's referred to as "cacum excrement," which the rabbit usually ingests directly from the anus. It contains vitally important vitamins and protein.

Precautions for Hot Days

Rabbits can't tolerate the heat, for they regulate their body temperature only through their ears and increased breathing. In the wild, the animals can retreat to their cool warrens at any time. Dwarf rabbits depend on us to take precautions, for otherwise they can experience heatstroke.

Outdoors Switch the time in the movable enclosure to the cooler morning hours and the early evening. Provide lots of well-ventilated, shady areas, including on the balcony (see p. 29).

Indoors If you don't have air-conditioning, you should air out the rabbits' room for a long time at night and draw the shades on south-facing windows during the day. Place some tiles in a corner of the cage and the indoor enclosure. They provide a cool surface to lie on.

Emergency Measures In case of breathing difficulties and circulatory weakness, you must immediately place a damp (but not ice-cold) hand towel over the animal. Change frequently until the condition has visibly improved. Do not bathe the rabbit, put it into a cold shower, or cool it with ice packs, or the overheated animal may have a stroke!

Caution: Maggots

As soon as it becomes warmer, flies are out and about, and they can be life threatening to rabbits.

Precautions My recommendations are more applicable than ever: Maintain absolute cleanliness in the accommodations and in the run (see p. 39). Thoroughly check over the rabbit's entire body every day (see p. 40). I have also put screens on my windows at home. Treat tiny wounds and injuries on the body with Swedish bitters or tincture of calendula (which disinfects and heals). Again, if you are unable to find these in stores, they can be purchased over the Internet. Trim away fur from the anal region that is smeared with droppings or wet with urine. Then spray the area with a solution of chamomile and dry it thoroughly. Rabbits with diarrhea, and weakened and overweight rabbits are at particular risk.

What Could Happen Flies lay their eggs on all soiled, damp, injured parts of the body. The larvae develop in a matter of hours, bore through the skin, and can literally eat the poor creature alive. As soon as you discover even a single maggot on your dwarf, take the afflicted rabbit to the veterinarian without delay.

Do Rabbits Need Shots?

As a rule, vaccines for rabbits are not commercially available in the United States, and are not administered on a routine basis.

Does Neutering Make Sense?

It's not appropriate to keep one rabbit by itself, and unchecked reproduction is irresponsible. Neutered animals mark and spray less, are easier to housebreak, and are overall more well balanced. Unneutered, sexually active rabbits would only suffer from pent-up drives.

Buck Have the buck neutered. Early neutering is recommended when the rabbit reaches sexual maturity (third to fourth month of life). That way the males don't start scrapping with one another, and you can even put a buck that was neutered early in with a female.

Doe In this instance, too, I generally recommend neutering animals kept as pets, for the following reasons:

› A female rabbit in heat can act quite aggressively toward others of the same sex.

› Even a neutered male may often be mounted and harried while the female is in heat.

› The risk of contracting uterine or ovarian cancer is as high as 80 percent.

› False pregnancy occurs more frequently.

It's normal for young animals to gain weight, but it's a cause for concern with adults. Rapid weight loss is also dangerous.

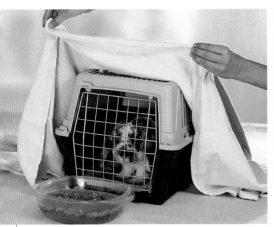

With respiratory infections, inhaling the aroma of chamomile blossoms (from a health food store) soaked in boiling water helps.

For heatstroke, place a moist towel over the animal. This lowers the body temperature.

Considerations The operation is more risky with a female and must be performed only at a veterinarian's office that has proven success in neutering female rabbits and uses inhalant anesthetics.

Before the Operation The rabbit should not fast, so that there is no additional strain on the sensitive digestive system. Since a dwarf cannot vomit, there is no danger of suffocation, as there is with dogs and cats. The rabbit can and should eat hay and light foods (apple, carrot, fennel) before the operation.

Precautions at Home In the first days, place the neutered animal in the hutch on cloths or paper to encourage healing. Bucks that have been neutered early can shortly be placed in with a female. A buck that has already mated or was neutered later on must be kept separate for about six additional weeks, or it may try to mate again. The male can also retain some sperm after the operation, and a female is ready to conceive right after giving birth. Rabbits commonly suffer from the cold after the operation. I place a heat lamp on the bars of the cage. That way I can place the rabbit under it as necessary.

Natural Remedies—the Home Drugstore

SWEDISH BITTERS A few drops on a wound disinfects and heals.

CHAMOMILE/THYME Loosens phlegm in the breathing organs and reduces inflammation when the rabbit inhales it.

EUPHRASIA EYEDROPS These help with red, irritated eyes.

Treating Rabbits Properly

For the territorial rabbit every change of location is at first stressful. Welcome your new arrival with a nicely set-up home and treat it with love right from the first days. That makes it easier for the little one to become acclimated, and builds trust in you.

Getting Started in Rabbit Life

When you pick up your animals, take the shortest way home. You can pick up rabbits easily and securely in a travel cage for small animals (see photo, p. 12). This type of carrier is also necessary when you visit the veterinarian.

Careful Acclimation

When you get home, immediately put the dwarf rabbits into the prepared indoor cage. Stay away for a couple of hours and let the animals explore their new home in peace. You can also sit there quietly, but don't take the animals out, carry them around, and pet them. This patient waiting is very difficult, especially for children. But particularly sensitive and somewhat shy animals would respond to an excessively boisterous welcome with a long-lasting retreat into their little house. Once the dwarfs start to groom themselves—something

that rabbits do only where they feel secure—or eat, then the first shock of moving is over.

Children Need Direction

From my own experience as a mother, and from continuous exchanges with my readers, I want to appeal to all parents not to leave sole responsibility for the dwarf rabbits to the children. Even schoolchildren and youths are very busy nowadays. And once the initial enthusiasm passes, the daily care for the animal is seen all too quickly as an annoying obligation, and the rabbits will become neglected. Read this guidebook with your children and support them in the daily duties so that the joy of having rabbits does not evaporate. Help your children set up the adventure playground (see pp. 24–25) and help them with the suggested ideas for keeping the rabbits occupied (see pp. 54

and 55). Children who grow up with animals and the support and participation of their parents are more social in their behavior, more responsible, and develop greater empathy. And this is an exceedingly valuable gift that you can give your child along the way.

A good team for a long time: With good care and a healthy diet, dwarf rabbits can live to the age of ten.

Building Trust

A rabbit's ability to remember is certainly not comparable to that of humans. Yet a rabbit is capable of connecting events and its own behavior with the resulting experiences and feelings. The animal instinctively will strive to have good, positive feelings, and to avoid as much as possible unpleasant, painful feelings by staying away from this situation (humans) or fighting against it. Your dwarf will always gladly come to you if you speak to it lovingly and reward it with a treat. But if someone frightens the animal, for example, by grabbing it unexpectedly from above, running after it, frightening it with loud noise, dropping it, or injuring it through handling, the rabbit will pull back from that person or defend itself aggressively. That's why it is so important to build trust every day and not destroy this trust, perhaps for a long time, through negligent or improper handling.

The Most Important Rules for Handling Rabbits

With their sharp senses and their inborn behavior as animals of flight, all rabbits react very sensitively to all forms of noise and hustle and bustle around them (see cage location, p. 22). If you observe the following basic rules, you and your little housemate will take more pleasure in each other and make a good team right from the start.

Making Contact Always approach a rabbit slowly and from the front. Speak to the dwarf with a friendly voice and then let it sniff your hand held out flat (see photo, right). If the rabbit behaves calmly, you can now stroke its back. Only with this preparation can you subsequently pick up the rabbit. Proper restraint is important, though. Failure to restrain the back legs of a rabbit when picked up can lead to the rabbit breaking its back when it kicks.

Developing Trust Right from the outset, offer special treats by hand. That way the dwarf learns to connect the hand and the owner with something pleasant, and will gladly come over to you. This hand feeding should also take place regularly during excursions outside the cage. If food is given exclusively inside the cage and in the bowl, you run the risk that a dominant rabbit will defend its food and territory aggressively.

Attention It's best to wait until the dwarf seeks closeness and physical contact with you. When you lie on the floor, perhaps the little one will come over and nudge you with its muzzle to communicate, "Hello, here I am, pat me." Now you can gently stroke the dwarf in the direction of the hair on its back, scratch its ears, or use your finger to stroke it from the back of its nose upward to the forehead. The rabbit's blissful, relaxed posture communicates to us that it enjoys our friendly physical attention, and many rabbits will even lick your hand (see How Rabbits "Talk," p. 7)

What Rabbits Don't Like Rabbits don't like to be tapped with fingertips or to be teased for fun in this way. Dwarf rabbits find stroking against the lay of the fur likewise unpleasant, and the same applies to fondling their lower body and touching their sensitive whiskers. Also, continually picking them up and forced cuddling greatly undermines their trust in you.

1 First always let the dwarf sniff your hand to see if it is already comfortable with your scent.

2 A dwarf rabbit prefers to choose cuddle time. Always pat the rabbit gently and with the lay of the hair.

3 My dwarf rabbits jump into a basket on command. A treat is helpful with this. That makes it easy to carry the dwarf.

4 Children should carry the dwarf in a basket and keep a hand securely on its back to keep it from jumping out.

Socializing Dwarf Rabbits

Ideally two littermates move together into the new home, and you take care of neutering early (see pp. 12 and 46). Or perhaps you have decided on a pair from an animal shelter (see Tips, p. 11). But what to do if your rabbit's life partner suddenly dies?

When a New Rabbit Moves In

How do I socialize a rabbit that has previously been kept alone, or is now alone, and get it used to a new partner?

The Right Partner Rabbits should be as close as possible in age. A young animal is not an appropriate match for an old one and could be excessively intimidated by it. Also, two dominant

animals that both want to have their way are not an ideal combination.

Moving In All rabbits are very territorial and live in an established pecking order. You must never make the mistake of simply putting a newcomer into a cage or run where another rabbit already lives. For acclimation and quarantine the new rabbit must spend about three weeks in its own indoor cage, preferably in a separate space.

The First Meeting

Rabbits recognize one another by a common family scent. It is helpful to rub a little secretion from the sex areas of the territory's occupant onto the palm of your hand (see Tips. p. 43) and then stroke it thoroughly onto the newcomer's fur.

Neutral Ground Choose a room in your house where neither of the rabbits has previously lived and marked out its territory. In the warm seasons you can also use the enclosure in the yard for letting the animals get used to one another.

Plenty of Room Around 35 square feet (10 sq. m) or more will allow the animals adequate area for flight.

Hiding Places Put some cardboard boxes, little houses (with two doorways), and tunnels into the room or the enclosure where an animal can take refuge if it feels too harried.

Food Scatter small treats, such as dandelions. That way the first meeting will leave a better taste in their mouths.

Happy as a pair: The dwarf cuddles with the lop and awaits a friendly grooming.

During this first encounter, the youngster dodges the attack with a jump into the air. It's a good thing rabbits are so agile.

Not so bad after all! After chasing each other around, the two lie close together as if nothing had happened.

War or Peace?

If you have followed all my advice, you can put the two rabbits into the meeting place. Now the trick is to keep your nerve and be patient. Many rabbits sniff each other and quickly make friends. It's also completely normal for the animals to chase each other around, jump wildly, and have little tussles (see photos on these two pages).

Attack But if the two keep biting each other violently, I recommend breaking it up. Throw a blanket over the fighters or try to interrupt things with a well-directed squirt from a water pistol. Then put the animals back into their individual cages and try again the next day.

Note: Don't use bare hands to separate the fighters. Any injuries will require treatment.

Partners in Anxiety Sometimes it helps to put the adversaries together into a travel cage and take them for an hour's ride in the car.

Housecleaning Everything should be cleaned thoroughly before putting compatible rabbits into their future home together. This at least establishes a "scent neutrality" and triggers no new conflicts.

My Experience I have been able to socialize all my rabbits regardless of age, sex, and breed. Of course my bucks are neutered, and the animals get plenty of exercise and stimulation. Lots of biting is the result of inadequate space and boredom.

And yet if one dwarf rabbit continually suffers because of another (frequently withdrawn, refusal to eat), then you should acknowledge this and keep the animals apart.

Stimulation for Activity and the Senses

Wild rabbits have to be very clever and active to assure their daily survival. A little program for keeping busy can only help your dwarf rabbits. It will keep their bodies fit and stimulate their senses. And as you can see, it has provided my little scamps with lots of pleasure.

1 Jumping Over Cans

Set up a row of full cans in the middle of the rabbit's enclosure (empty cans would tip over too easily). To keep the dwarf from running around the ends of the obstacle, I close off the sides with boxes and little houses. Now the row of cans works like a natural barrier, and the little one spontaneously jumps over.
Notes: Provide a nonslip surface to protect the rabbit's joints.

2 A Homemade Hurdle

A simple hurdle is screwed to a base plate (30 x 10 inches / 75 x 25 cm; the top slat is 16 inches / 40 cm long, and the side supports are 8 inches / 20 cm high). If any little sneaks at first crawl under it, you can cover the hurdle with cardboard.

3 A Grass Nest for Chewing Fun

Pet shops sell round sleeping nests made from woven grass for hamsters. Fill one with hay. My two dwarf lops had fun rolling the ball around and plucking the hay from the holes. It's no problem if the grass nest gets gnawed, since it is made from natural materials.

4 Rustle Box

Fill a shoe box with crumpled paper towels, napkins, or toilet paper. My dwarfs love to rustle around in this box and jump in and out, and they often take a nap in their rustle box.

5 The Wandering Carrot

Tie a piece of carrot (or some other treat) to a string and lure the animal slowly out of its little house or through a tunnel.

6 A Chew Tree

This is something that I invented and that has been reproduced countless times. A small forked tree branch a little over a foot (34 cm) high is screwed onto a plywood plate (16 inches / 40 cm in diameter). Drill holes at various heights in the branch and stick in vegetables, fruit, or twigs. As in the wild, the rabbit now has to work for its food.

Information: **Behavior and Activity**

FITNESS It's healthier for a dwarf rabbit to jump frequently over low obstacles than to try to set a record for high jumping.

PLAYTIME By nature rabbits are active in the early morning and the evening.

FOOD MOTIVATION This works only when the dwarf is sufficiently hungry.

Training and Housebreaking

Dwarf rabbits that live indoors should be housebroken. Most owners desire this, and many rabbits can be trained to a certain degree. But don't be too disappointed if something occasionally "misses the target." By nature dwarf rabbits are clean animals, but they also have a natural need to mark their territory with droppings and urine.

Elimination

Dwarfs usually use a corner of their cage as a toilet. You can put in a plastic bowl and fill it with small-animal bedding or straw pellets (see p. 22). I don't use a toilet in the rabbit hutch anymore, but rather only in the indoor enclosure, and my tips apply to this as well.

› During excursions the cage door remains open so that the animals can use their toilet corner in the cage if they need to.

› At first, limit the excursions outside the cage; this encourages housebreaking.

› Rabbits prefer to leave their droppings and urine in corners; they especially like dark places. Place the toilet box in the location that the animals choose for themselves.

› Common cat litter boxes with a cover (but no swinging door) or a rim (see photo, p. 59) are good choices. The little scamps can also dig in it, or spread the litter all around the room.

› Put a little straw and some droppings from the "slop corner" in the cage into the toilet.

› Watch your rabbit closely. If it's getting ready to piddle—by slightly lifting its rear end—say curtly and clearly, in a sharp tone of voice, "No!" or "Yuck!" Then carefully place the animal into its toilet or guide it there.

This homemade "suspension bridge" provides some variety in the outdoor pen. Rabbits like elevated observation posts.

> If the dwarf does its business in the box, praise it by saying, "Good bunny!"
> Repeat the exercise regularly.
> Collect any droppings that miss the mark and put them into the box. Thoroughly wash any droplets of urine that hit the rug. Peppermint or lemon oil dissolved in water will mask the urine smell and prevent a repeat.

Note: You must never shove a rabbit's nose into its droppings. The animal would not understand the connection. Also any type of scolding or a slap on the bottom would only upset the dwarf rabbit.

Picking Up and Carrying

The little creatures prefer to hop independently, at will, between the cage and their exercise enclosure. That's why I recommend the combination cage/indoor enclosure (see pp. 24–25). Rabbits prefer this to always being set in and out by their owner. I have trained my animals to go into their cage on command. I stand behind the rabbits, clap my hands twice, say, "Hop, hop into your hutch," and soon they are all in. My little rascals learned that very quickly, because they know that there is some delicious food waiting for them in their cage for their good behavior.

Neck Grip The preparatory contact must be made (see p. 51) before you pick up a dwarf. Then you grasp the animal with your right hand on the loose neck fur behind the ears. To pick up the rabbit immediately support the hind part and the legs with the left hand. At no time must the animal hang unsupported; otherwise it will start wild, panicked efforts to get loose. Picking up a rabbit by the ears is cruelty to animals!

Vacationing with Rabbits

TIPS FROM THE
RABBIT EXPERT
Monika Wegler

TAKING THEM ALONG Riding in a car and changes in location and climate add up to stress for dwarf rabbits. However, you could bring the animals with you if you are spending your vacation in a house for a fairly long time.

LEAVING THEM HOME This is what the rabbits like best. Arrange early for an experienced caregiver during your vacation, whom you can introduce to the chores in good time. Prepare a list for the rabbit sitter containing all the care required and the habits of your dwarf rabbits, plus the veterinarian's phone number.

BOARDING FACILITY Find out which boarding kennels also accept small animals. I recommend that you be totally convinced in advance that the rabbits will be housed properly and well cared for.

SAD BUT TRUE It still happens that countless rabbits are simply let loose as a cheap and quick solution before vacation time. If you ever find an abandoned animal, bring it to an animal shelter.

Cat Grasp This hold requires a little practice, but it's more comfortable for the rabbit. I photographed this method of picking up and carrying a rabbit on page 13. The chest and hind end are supported, and the front and back paws are held securely with the fingers. To prevent excessive squeezing, the index finger of the hand is placed between the rabbit's legs.

Carrying The rabbit sits on the bent left forearm, and many rabbits like to cuddle in the bend of the arm. The right hand remains lying on the animal's neck. That way you can pet the rabbit calmly as you carry it, or if it becomes restless, you can immediately grasp it securely.

Into the Basket Not only children, but also many adults, as I continually see, have problems with picking up and carrying rabbits securely. With the help of little treats, I have trained my rabbits to jump into a little basket (see photo, p. 51). That is a secure way to carry a rabbit; here, too, the right hand always rests on the rabbit's back in case it's needed. This is important, so that the rabbit doesn't suddenly jump out and injure itself.

The red dwarf named Pumpernickel devotedly licks the lion-headed dwarf lop Whisker's ears. You can see the tongue clearly.

A Guinea Pig as a Companion

Many rabbit owners think they are doing their dwarf a favor when they put in a guinea pig as a roommate. But the pets are very different in their behavior, their body language, and their needs. At most the two of them form a type of forced association that is characterized by permanent misunderstandings—as if one spoke only Chinese and the other only Russian. The reason often proposed, that "they cuddle so nicely with each other" is, regrettably, nothing but an incorrect interpretation on the part of the humans. Often there are also attacks in which the rabbit can seriously injure the defenseless guinea pig. Let your dwarf live with another rabbit right from the start. That's the only way the rabbit can satisfy its multifaceted social requirements. And a guinea pig would rather live with another guinea pig!

Living with Dogs and Cats

Rabbits are prey and flight animals. When they live with "predators," there are inevitable misunderstandings, and many times harmless fooling around ends up with dire consequences.

Cats When a playful cat pounces on a rabbit or gallops through the house, it's no fun at all for the rabbit. Large, pugnacious rabbits know how to defend themselves by biting, but all too quickly a

blow from a paw lands in the rabbit's eye, or the dwarf runs into something in its panic.

Dogs Of course dogs can be trained to obedience more effectively than cats so that they don't send the rabbit into a panic with their loud barking. But even in this case a playful snap or push by the dog may even cost the little dwarf rabbit its life.

Note: Don't leave a cat or a dog with a rabbit without supervision!

Fill the litter box with pellets made from natural fibers. They are especially absorbent.

Clubs and Associations

American Rabbit Breeders
Association, Inc.
P.O. Box 5667
Bloomington, IL 61702
(309) 664-7500
ARBAPOST@aol.com

House Rabbit Society
International Headquarters &
Rabbit Center
148 Broadway
Richmond, CA 94804
(510) 970-7575
www.rabbit.org

Questions about Dealing with Rabbits

can be directed to your local pet shop, or you can do research online.

Important Notes

> **Injuries** In dealing with dwarf rabbits, it is possible to experience bites and scratches. Have such injuries looked at by a doctor.

> **Allergies** People who have allergies to animal hair should consult with a doctor before getting a rabbit.

> **Accidental shock** To prevent potentially fatal electric shocks, make sure that your dwarf rabbit does not chew on any electrical cords.

Additional Internet Addresses

(these contain information on care, housing, health, poisonous plants, adoption, and links to other rabbit sites)

American Rabbit Breeders
Association (ARBA)
www.arba.net

House Rabbit Society (HRS)
www.rabbit.org

American Netherland Dwarf Rabbit
Club
www.andrc.com

Mini Lop Rabbit Club of America
www.miniloprabbit.com

National Mini Rex Rabbit Club
www.nmrrc.com

American Society for the Prevention
of Cruelty to Animals (ASPCA)
www.aspca.org

Veterinary Partners
(information on health care)
www.veterinarypartners.com

Information about poisonous plants
in the house and yard:
www.thegardehelper.com/
toxichouse.htm
www.hsus.org/pets/pet_care/
protect_your_pet_from_common_
household_dangers/common_
poisonous_plants.html

About building a rabbit enclosure:
www.rabbit.org/journal/1/
place-space-update.html

MAGAZINES

Rabbits USA
Mission Viejo, CA
www.animalnetwork.com

BOOKS

Gendon, Karen. 2000. *The Rabbit Handbook.* Hauppauge, NY: Barron's Educational Series.

Harriman, Marinell. 2005. *House Rabbit Handbook: How to Live with an Urban Rabbit, 4th edition.* Alameda, CA: Drollery Press.

McBride, Anne. 1998. *Why Does My Rabbit...?* London: Souvenir Press.

Moore, Lucile C. 2005. *A House Rabbit Primer: Understanding and Caring for Your Companion Rabbit.* Santa Monica, CA: Santa Monica Press.

Pavia, Audrey. 2003. *Rabbits for Dummies.* Hoboken, NJ: Wiley Publishing, Inc.

Viner, Bradley. 1999. *All About Your Rabbit.* Hauppauge, NY: Barron's Educational Series, Inc.

Wegler, Monica. 2008. *My Dwarf Rabbit.* (My Pet series). Hauppauge, NY: Barron's Educational Series, Inc.

First edition for the United States, its territories, and dependencies and Canada published in 2008 by Barron's Educational Series, Inc.
German edition by:
Monika Wegler
Published originally under the title:
Zwergkaninchen in the series, *GU Tierratgeber*
©2007 by Grafe und Unzer Verlag GmbH
Munich, Germany

English translation © Copyright 2008 by Barron's Educational Series, Inc.
English translation by Eric A. Bye, M.A.

All inquiries should be addressed to:
Barron's Educational Series, Inc.
250 Wireless Blvd.
Hauppauge, NY 11788
www.barronseduc.com

ISBN−10: 0-7641-3926-6
ISBN−13: 978-0-7641-3926-0

Library of Congress Catalog No.: 2008003554

Library of Congress Cataloging-in-Publication Data:
Wegler, Monika.
  [Zwergkaninchen. English]
  Dwarf rabbits : everything about purchase, care, nutrition, behavior, and training / Monika Wegler.
      p. cm. — (A complete pet owner's manual)
  Includes index.
  ISBN-13: 978-0-7641-3926-0
  ISBN-10: 0-7641-3926-6
  1. Dwarf rabbits. I. Title.
  SF455.D85W4513 2008
  636.932'2—dc22
                                    2008003554

Printed and bound in China

9 8 7 6 5 4 3 2 1

The Author and Photographer

Monika Wegler has worked since 1983 as a freelance photographer and author in Munich, Germany. She has illustrated more than fifty-five successful animal handbooks, many of which she wrote herself. She has become well known through her highly esteemed calendars and publications in periodicals and advertising, in addition to her work with books. She has more than twenty-five years of practical experience in owning and raising rabbits. Mrs. Wegler keeps animals, lives with them, and for many years has actively and financially helped animal welfare organizations, whose work she knows well. If you want to know more about the author and photographer, you can visit her web page: www.wegler.de. All photos in this handbook are by her.

SOS – what to do?

A Shy Rabbit

PROBLEM: The rabbit won't let you catch it, and keeps hiding. RECOMMENDATION: Set up the cage in an elevated place, take away the little house, and use only a cloth on the roof of the cage. Don't force attention onto the rabbit. Feed treats by hand.

Gnawing the Cage

PROBLEM: The dwarf rabbit pulls and gnaws on the bars of the cage, and runs around restlessly inside the cage. RECOMMENDATION: Provide more time outside the cage, and companionship with another rabbit in case the rabbit lives alone. Hang twigs high on the bars of the cage so that the rabbit can keep busy gnawing.

Mounting the Other Rabbit

PROBLEM: The doe constantly mounts another doe or even a neutered male. RECOMMENDATION: With two females it may help to get them socialized with a neutered buck. If the female tends toward a state of continually being in heat, neutering as a health measure is advisable.

Old Bites Young

PROBLEM: A female has a new young buck as a partner and attacks it so that it is now totally terrified. RECOMMENDATION: With this difference in age, the little one is off to a fairly bad start. Rabbits have no "puppy tolerance," as dogs do. Place the young animal into its own cage so it can begin by calming down. Begin reintroducing the animals on neutral ground (see p. 52). Be patient: The little one will grow, become more confident, and eventually make friends with the female. Don't overlook timely neutering (see p. 46).

Destructive Mania

PROBLEM: The dwarf rabbits gnaw everything in the house. They dig holes in the carpet. RECOMMENDATION: Connect the cage to the recommended indoor enclosure (see pp. 24–25). The dwarfs can fulfill their need to dig and gnaw to their hearts' content in this adventure playground. This protects the house.